ME AND THE PANDEMIC

VEER BATHIJA

ISBN 979-888555681-1

A NOTE FROM THE READER

IT IS A PLEASURE FOR ME TO WRITE THIS
BOOK

I HOPE YOU LIKE THIS BOOK BECAUSE THIS
IS MY FIRST BOOK

NAME_______________________________

AGE____________________

ADDRESS_____________________________________

PLACE WHERE BOOK WAS
BOUGHT____

PLEASE EMAIL IT TO

veersexperiments2020@gmail.com

IT WILL BE A GREAT HELP OF YOU

About author

Name-VEER BATHIJA

Age-12

Book#1

Book Name-Me And The Pandemic

HOPE YOU LIKE THIS BOOK

LET'S START THE STORY

Me And The Pandemic

VEER BATHIJA

THE STORY BEGINS

1

THE BEGINNING

COVID HIT INDIA IN December 2019.

SO IT STARTED WHEN I WAS IN MY SCHOOL OUR MAM ANNOUNCED THAT THERE WAS A KIND OF FLU IN OUR COUNTRY IT WAS CALLED COVID-19 WE TOOK OUR NAPKINS AND WE PUT IT IN OUR FACE BECAUSE THEY TOLD THAT THERE WAS A 1ST CASE NEAR US SO THAT'S HOW IT ALL STARTED..

Now the next day we had sports day, me and my friend were waiting because the school told that it may get canceled so they told it is canceled and they started telling us to go back home i thought that it was a small flu because i was in 3rd grade that time when i came home i got to know it is a

small virus like chickenpox but now omg i can't
tell one day 10000 cases of covid-19

Then there was a invention called online classes
that time i was very small so i thought just a
few days More till date i am hoping for the same

But it is 2 and half years since online classes.In
online class one child was in unmute by mistake
so he told mom give me my book mom told class
is started come and take the book i will hit you
with slipper mom left the class there were many
things like that

2

INVENTION OF MASK

And then was the invention of mask

Types of masks;

N95 mask

Cloth mask

paper mask

3 layers mask

10 rs mask

50rs mask

and the main

surgical mask

ect

AND NEW RULES WHICH WE HAVE TO FOLLOW LIKE

;

WHERE MASK FULL TIME (WHEN OUTSIDE)

USE SANITIZER FREQUENTLY

SANITIZE ALL THINGS COMING FROM

OUTSIDE

OMG!!!!!!! SO MANY

3

VACCINATION

NOW IT WAS A WHILE SINCE THEY WERE TELLING ABOUT VACATION

BUT IT HAS STILL NOT COME FOR ADULTS AND KIDS I AM TALKING ABOUT PAST NOW VACCINATION HAS COME

But now they were telling that the vaccination will come after 2 years but finally the vaccination came

AFTER everybody started taking the vaccination the covid-19 reduced a bit but again after some days

agin it is

rased

Then there was a news that if you take the vaccination in next 2 years you will die but then

we found out it was fake!!!!!!!!!!!!!!!!!!!!

then my mom and dad got the first dose of vacation and then they had hand pain ect for

3-4 days and then they were fine

After

couple of months it was the time for second dose of vacation

was taken and thennnn! agin hand pain for 3-4 days then they where fine and now they are perfect

$$4$$

DIFFICULTY OF STUDENTS

NOW IN ONLINE CLASS THEY ARE MANY DIFFICULTY IN LIFE

If i start listing them it will take a lot of time but i will still list some of them

SEE OFLINE CLASS ARE THE BEST FOR ME.

IF I TELL YOU SERIOUSLY I HATE ONLINE CLASS.

BECAUSE WHEN I ATTEND ONLINE CLASS IT IS VERY DIFFERENT

I SOMETIMES THINK THAT WHAT IS COVID-19 AND WHY IS THIS HAPPENING

I CAN'T ENJOY SCHOOL LIFE?

I HOPE ALL MY SCHOOL TEACHERS READ THIS BOOK

Types of DIFFICULTY

LESS MARKS

NETWORK

TIME

HOME WORK

SCREEN TIME

CLASS LEAVE AND RE JOIN

MAM ABCET FULL CLASS GONE

NOT ABLE TO STUDY BECAUSE OF

NETWORK ISSUE

BACKGROUND VOICE

CHILDREN SCREAMING

HEADACHE

OMG!!!

ECT!!!!!!!!!!!!!!!!!!!!!!!!!!!!!!!1

*BEFORE;FIRST I USED TO WAKE UP A 6AM
BECAUSE THE BUS USED TO*

COME AT 7;15

NOW;NO BUS I WAKE UP AT 9;30-10;00

BEFORE;

5

CHANGE OF WORK LIFE OF PARENTS

FIRST I USED TO GO TO SCHOOL AND MOM & DAD AT OFFICE

And i used to go to daycare tell mom & dad come home and then i come home and eat dinner

and next day again same

This was our daily routine

I HATED THIS I TOLD MOM

I can't bare this in daycare for 5 hours in 4 walls

Then i left daycare and go home and then go to tuition and then i used to play tell mom & dad come back

this was still ok

MY MOM GAVE ME ONE MORE OPTION THAT MY MOM WILL QUIT I TOLD NO YOU CONTINUE

But now fully work from home

online school

online guitar

online tuition

omg!!!!!!!!!!!!!!!!!!!!!!!!

ect!!!!!!!!!!!!!!!!!!!!!!!!

6

GADGETS AND FAMILY

Our Families always wanted to keep us away

from Gadgets. But the world changed and everything was on Gadgets.

Can witness every family member's life was Mobile.

School Online Classes on Computer / Laptop.

Parents WFH from their Laptops

Elders of Family kept themselves occupied with their mobiles.

Grandparents learnt how to operate the mobile.

Video calls were in trend since travel was cut. Families used to unite in the Video Calls.

Amazon Prime, Netflix, Disney, SonyLiv, Zee5 were the only time pass for weekend or for the ones who were quarantined.

ONLINE VISITS;

EVEN DOCTOR VISIT IS ONLINE

SCHOOL 100%

OFFICE CALLS

COOKING

GUITAR

TESTS

EVEN RESULTS

OMG!!!!!!!!!!!!!!!!!!!!!!!!!!!!!!!!!!!

7

HOW MODI TOOK COVID-19 FORWARD

IT WAS FIRST WHEN MODI JI GAVE A SPEECH THAT THERE IS A FIRST WAVE OF COVID-19&LOCKDOWN

IT WAS FIRST WHEN MODI JI GAVE A SPEECH AND TOLD .PM Modi called for 'janata curfew' on March 22 from 7 AM-9 PM

THIS WAS THE FIRST CURFEW IN INDIA JAY HIND JAY HIND

But now there are many variants of covid-19 like:

COVID-19

DELTA

OMICRON

ECT!!!!!!!!

They told only take away

in restaurants that to only 6AM-12PM

And the best

NO MASK

NO ENTRY

6FT SOCIAL DISTANCING

GROCERIES ONLY 6AM-12PM

*A DAY WHEN MODI JI TOLD THAT TAKE
BELLS AND LAMPS AND RING IT IN THE
BALCONY*

AND TELL GO CORONA GO

AND IT SEEMED TO BE A GREAT RESULT

*BUT NOW GOD KNOWS WHEN SCHOOL WILL
REOPEN*

8

SUMMERY

THIS BOOK IS ALL ABOUT PANDEMIC AND HOW WE FACED THE COVID 19 AND LOCKDOWN

ALL ABOUT COVID-19 AND VIRUS

IT IS MY FIRST BOOK AND IT IS A PLEASURE TO WRITE AND I HOPE YOU ALL LIKED THIS BOOK

PLS GIVE IT ALL THE SUPPORT AND LOVE

PART 2 COMING SOON

THANK YOU FOR PURCHASING THIS BOOK

www.ingramcontent.com/pod-product-compliance
Lightning Source LLC
Chambersburg PA
CBHW070000180726
48002CB00018B/1582